Table of Contents

Rourke Educational Media
A Division of Carson Dellosa Education
rourkeeducationalmedia.com

Can you find these words?

fruits

groom

hug

tool

What Do Chimps Do?

Chimpanzees are apes.
They live in Africa.

Chimps eat many things.

They like **fruits**, seeds, and eggs.

A chimp can use a **tool**!

Chimps use sticks to poke and dig.

Chimps live together.
They laugh and **hug**.

hug

Chimps **groom** each other.

Friends remove bugs and dirt.

Chimps talk!

They grunt and use hand signs.

Did you find these words?

They like **fruits**, seeds, and eggs.

Chimps **groom** each other.

They laugh and **hug**.

A chimp can use a **tool**!

Photo Glossary

fruits (froots): The parts of flowering plants that have seeds. Apples, grapes, and melons are fruits.

groom (groom): To clean, brush, and take care of the body of an animal or human.

hug (hug): To show love by putting your arms around someone.

tool (tool): A device that helps someone do work. Hammers and axes are tools.

Index

About the Author

Lisa Jackson is a writer from Ohio. She would like to visit Africa someday, especially to see its amazing animals. For now, she likes to feed the giraffes at the Columbus Zoo!

www.rourkeeducationalmedia.com

PHOTO CREDITS: Cover ©USO; Pg 2, 10, 14, 15 ©PhilDarby; Pg 2, 4, 14, 15 ©wrangel; Pg 2, 6, 14, 15 ©markrhiggins; Pg 2, 8, 14, 15 ©Windzepher; Pg 3 ©ANDREYGUDKOV; Pg 12 ©abadonian

Edited by: Keli Sipperley
Cover and interior design by: Rhea Magaro-Wallace

Library of Congress PCN Data
Chimpanzee / Lisa Jackson
(African Animals)
ISBN 978-1-73160-560-3 (hard cover)(alk. paper)
ISBN 978-1-73160-446-0 (soft cover)
ISBN 978-1-73160-609-9 (e-Book)
ISBN 978-1-73160-683-9 (ePub)
Library of Congress Control Number: 2018967317

Printed in the United States of America,
North Mankato, Minnesota